CW00421268

ish Short walks
in north Cornwall

Paul White

Bossiney Books · Exeter

This updated reprint 2023. First published 2004 by
Bossiney Books Ltd, 68 Thorndale Courts, Whitycombe Way, Exeter, EX4 2NY
www.bossineybooks.com
Copyright © 2004 Paul White All rights reserved
ISBN 978-1-915664-04-4

Acknowledgements
The maps are by Graham Hallowell, cover design by Heards Design Partnership,
photographs by the author. The publishers are grateful to Laurence Smith
for checking the walks prior to this reprint.
The boots on the front cover were kindly supplied by The Brasher Boot Company.

Printed in Great Britain by Deltor, Satash, PL12 6LZ

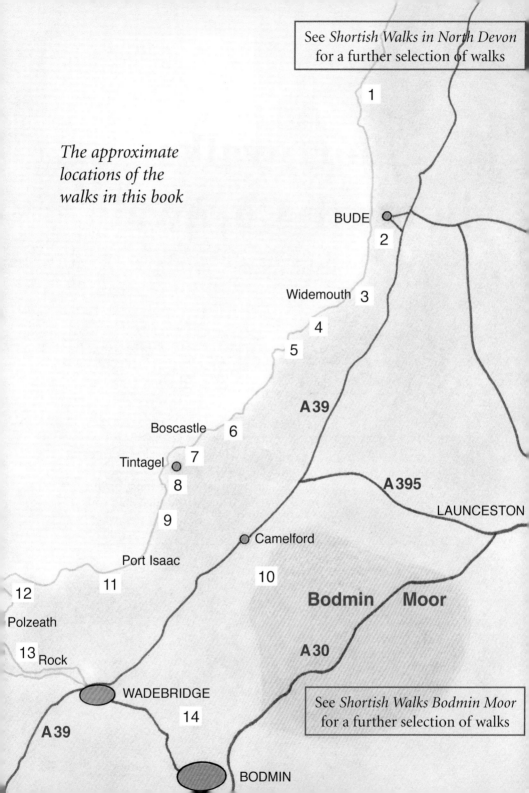

Introduction

For ease of understanding we have defined 'north Cornwall' in this book as the area east of the Camel estuary and north of the A30. A companion volume has been published – *Shortish Walks Bodmin Moor*. If these walks are too long, try *Really Short Walks North Cornwall*.

A 'shortish' walk is intended to take a couple of hours or so, and is typically 6-8 km (4-5 miles) in length. How long you actually take will depend on your fitness, enthusiasm, and the weather conditions. All the walks are circular, and the majority involve a section of the coast path with a rural return. There are two wholly inland walks.

Safety

Cliff walking can be very exposed; the wind-chill factor is like being out in the Atlantic, and of course Cornish weather can change very rapidly, so you need to carry extra layers of clothing, as well as waterproofs, for what is often an abrupt change of temperature between inland and cliff walking.

Many of the walks involve fairly strenuous ascents and descents, especially on the coast path. Proper walking boots are vital for grip and ankle support, and a walking pole or stick is useful for balance in the descents. On the inland sections in particular you may well find muddy patches even in dry weather, not to mention briars, thistles and nettles, all of which thrive in our soil, so bare legs are a liability.

The main hazard of walking the cliff path is that for most of the way it is not fenced off from the drop. Go no nearer the edge than you have to: you might be standing on an overhang. Take great care when the path does take you near the edge, and keep a close eye on children and dogs. In some places the cliffs are eroding, so respect diversions.

The maps provided in this book look very attractive but they are only intended as sketch maps, so you may well want to carry an OS 1:25,000 map. OS grid references are given where needed.

The Cornish countryside

Despite many pressures on their livelihoods, Cornish farmers are still trying to make a living from the land you pass through. Please respect their crops; if a few of them haven't yet restored the route of the footpath through their fields, no doubt they'll do so 'd'rec'ly', so go round the edge of the field! Leave gates closed or open as you find them, and keep dogs under control, especially during the lambing season.

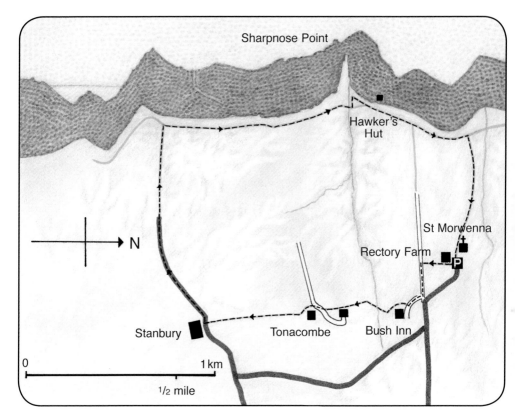

Walk 1 Morwenstow

Distance: 5.8 km (3 1/2 miles) Time: 2 hours OS Explorer sheet 126
Character: A pleasant inland section, then stunning coastline, famous
as the home of Parson Robert Hawker – minor Victorian poet, first-rate
eccentric, and rescuer of shipwrecked corpses. One very steep descent
and ascent on coast path; vertiginous in places.

Park at Morwenstow Church (SS 206153), where Rectory Farm offers
excellent refreshments in season. Walk up past the front of the farm,
through a gate (FOOTPATH TO TIDNA VALLEY), over a stile and across a
field to a gated stile. Turn left along the track (CROSSTOWN).

  Bear right when you come to the green and head across to the Bush
Inn. A footpath runs immediately to the right of the inn, then cuts
diagonally across the beer garden to a gap in the far left corner. Go
through a gate then descend to another gate, which leads into the valley. Descend the steps then turn left and cross a stream. Walk up what
looks like an ancient packhorse track.

  Proceed in a more or less straight line through gates, then bear left
to a woodland path. After another gate, cross a farm track and go

through the gate ahead, passing Tonacombe, a Tudor manor house with a rather grand gateway.

Proceed through another gate and climb the field edge on the left and the cross-field path until you reach a stile at the top with gates either side (watch out for a tricky sloping stone as you descend from the stile). Then cross the field ahead: you will see the strange shapes of the GCHQ 'radio station' emerging above the crop. Go through a gate, cross a stile into a lane, and turn right. (The farm is Stanbury, and is again Tudor and in part even earlier.)

Pass two useful car parks, not shown on the OS map, and keep straight on, signed PUBLIC FOOTPATH. After a number of gates, turn right along the coast path.

Pass the dramatic promontory called Sharpnose Point (see photo above). After entering National Trust land at Tidna Shute, keep left up steps at a path junction. Climb very steeply for 200 m, gaining 80 m in altitude in that distance!

Ignore a path on the right and continue through a kissing-gate. On the left is Hawker's Hut, where the vicar contemplated the ocean and smoked opium. Return to the main path, and continue until you can see the church tower on your right. Cross a field back to your car.

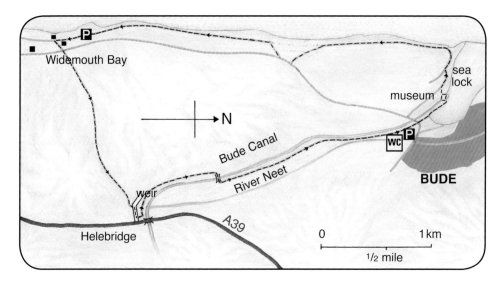

Walk 2   Widemouth & Bude

Distance: 9.2 km (5³/₄ miles)   Time: 2¹/₄ hours   OS Explorer sheet 111
Character: Easy walking: pleasant farmland, then the Bude Canal
which is quite unlike any other Cornish landscape, then low clifftops.

You could start this walk from the car park by the Bude Visitor Centre, but I prefer to park in the (currently free) car park just north of the Beach House Shop at Widemouth Bay (SS 199032). This saves the cliff scenery for the end of the walk.

From the back of the car park, take the path south, towards the beach and parallel to the road. Pass seaward of one house, then at the second house turn left, up to the road. Cross 'Marine Drive' and take the PUBLIC FOOTPATH opposite, which is a well-beaten path.

After 1.8 km this emerges on a track. Turn right, and before crossing the stream turn left – there is no need to go onto the main road. Join the towpath and follow it for 2.5 km, crossing the canal mid-way, till you reach a car park (toilets and Visitor Centre). Cross the busy road at the road bridge and continue down the right bank. To your right is the Castle Heritage Centre, with a museum and café.

Cross the canal at the sea-lock, turn right, climb steps to a road and continue to more steps, at the top of which you turn right onto the COAST PATH. Follow this as far as the road at Upton, turn right along the pavement for about 200 m, then turn right again on COAST PATH – WANSON MOUTH back to Widemouth Bay.

> The Bude Canal was opened in 1823, and its purpose was to take sea-sand inland as agricultural fertiliser.

Above: Bude breakwater
Below: A lock on the Bude Canal between Helebridge and Bude

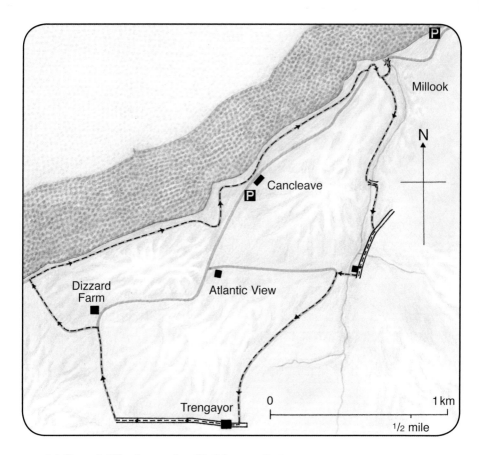

Walk 3 Millook, south of Widemouth Bay

Distance: 8.3km (5¹/4 miles) Time: 2¹/4 hours OS Explorer sheet 111
Character: A very fine walk – perhaps the only one in this book where the coastal section can (in the right conditions) be bettered by the inland section: magical woodland.
On the downside, the holloway section is likely to be muddy even after a drought, so after rain it can be seriously muddy!

Park at Cancleave, 1km south of Millook on the coast road, where there is space for 4 cars (SX176992). The easiest approach is from Wainhouse Corner. (If you're starting from Widemouth, there's a car park just north of Millook: that adds a substantial ascent and descent to the walk, but has the considerable advantage that you don't have to do the tricky drive from there to Cancleave.)

From Cancleave, start by walking out to the coast path and turning right. Follow it to Millook, and walk down the lane to take a look at the beach, which has some remarkable geology – 'chevron folding'.

From the beach, walk back up the lane to the first corner, where a track (PUBLIC FOOTPATH) leads inland. After 1 km, when the track crosses a stream by a concrete bridge, cross the neighbouring footbridge and turn right through woodland at the Woodland Trust sign.

This leads to a path through a meadow, full of wild flowers in Spring and Summer. Leave the meadow at the far left side and turn right along the track towards DIZZARD & TRENGAYOR. Pass the back of a house and turn right through a kissing gate; cross a footbridge, climb a few steps and turn left.

After winding through more beautiful woodland the path ascends a holloway – an ancient road, sometimes muddy as they always tend to be. At the top of the holloway go through a gate and turn right along a track, past a farm (gates) and out to a lane.

Turn right and after 420 m turn left, TO THE COASTPATH. Pass through two gates and keep left down a track. From a field gate a path leads down the right side of two fields to a footbridge.

Cross and turn right, steeply uphill through a wood. On entering a field, keep the hedge on your right, heading north-west. At the top, turn right across a kissing gate then immediately left through another kissing gate, TO COAST PATH. Keep to the right of a boggy area, then descend the field with the hedge on your left.

A short path from a gate at the bottom corner of the field leads out to the coast path. Turn right, and follow the path back to Cancleave.

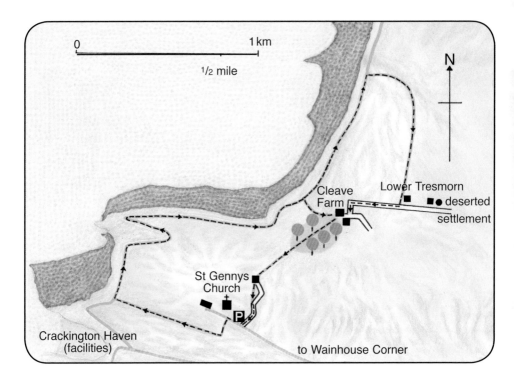

Walk 4   St Gennys

Distance: 6 km (3 3/4 miles) Time: 2 hours OS Explorer sheet 111
Can be shortened to 3.6 km, but still strenuous.
Character: Dramatic cliff scenery, with steep descents and ascents.

St Gennys Churchtown lies just north of Crackington Haven (where refreshments and toilets are available) and is approached from Wainhouse Corner on the A39. There is parking space for several cars on the road above the church (SX 149972).

Walk towards the cottages, then at the National Trust sign take the footpath to the left (COASTAL FOOTPATH). Go up steps and through a kissing gate, then keep the hedge on your right across a large field, ignoring the gates to the right. A gate at the far end of the field takes you out onto the cliff, and to the coast path. Turn right along it.

Before long the path starts to descend, nearly to sea level, and then to climb the opposite side of the valley. At the top it briefly follows a ridge with a drop to either side – not really dangerous except in a gale, but some people may feel vertigo (see photograph opposite).

After a further 600 m go through a gate, then cross a stile. Immediately after the stile turn sharp left, past another stile which has lost its fence, and follow the cliff edge.

10

At the sign LOWER TRESMORN you could take a short cut. To do that, don't pass the field hedge but turn right along it, and after 130 m you'll come to the fingerpost indicated as (*) in the text below.

For the full walk continue along the cliff path. Cross a footbridge and continue over the next crest. When you reach a wire fence, don't go through the gate but turn right. Keep the fence on your left round two sides of the field, leaving the field at the top left by a gate. A metal gate ahead of you leads into a track which after 400 m brings you to Lower Tresmorn Farm. At the farmyard, turn right through a gate and immediately left along the field edge to another gate.

For a diversion to see the remains of a deserted medieval settlement turn left along the track and you'll emerge on a gravelled area; ahead you'll see paddocks full of humps and bumps. That's it!

Otherwise after going through the gate turn right along the track, which abruptly turns left and down through a gate to Cleave Farm. Turn right (FOOTPATH) past 'The Barn', along a tarmac track and to the right of 'Abel's', and to a fingerpost. (*)

Turn left (CHURCH), cross a stile and after 60 m bear left and cross a stile (CHURCH) into a path downhill through sheltered woodland. Cross the stream and turn right.

You will emerge in a largish field with a house on the far side. Head just to the left of the house and you will find a stile crossing onto a track, then footpath, then track again, which leads uphill back to the church car park.

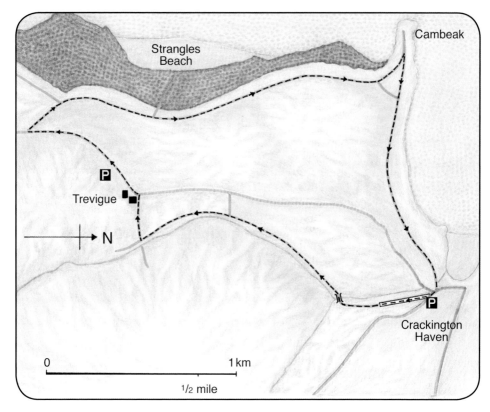

Walk 5   Crackington Haven

Distance: 7.3km (4½ miles)   Time: 2 hours   OS Explorer sheet 111
Character: Attractive woodland, then spectacular coast. Numerous
butterfly species in Summer.

Park at Crackington Haven (SX 143968), where there are cafés and
beach shops, toilets and a pub. There is an alternative starting point
just south of Trevigue (SX 135951), with free parking but no facilities.

Turn left out of the car park. Go up the road past the turning to
Trevigue, then turn right opposite 'Coombe Cottages' along FOOTPATH
TO EAST WOOD.

It starts as a private road, then after a gate becomes a path. Cross a
stream and after 30 m turn right towards SHEEPDIP. Follow the path up
the valley for 700 m: keep left (SHEEPDIP) and after a further 650 m at
a crossing of paths turn right (to TREVIGUE).

Climb up to Trevigue, where a gate just above the former farmhouse
(now holiday lets in grounds lovingly manicured by the National
Trust) leads you out onto a lane. Turn left and after 600 m (having

12

ignored one right turn through a kissing gate) turn right at a kissing gate which is easy to miss. The footpath goes diagonally across a field, holding the contour, to another kissing gate. Turn right along the coast path (CRACKINGTON HAVEN) and continue for 1.5 km.

At a fork keep left (yellow arrow) and left again, up the side of Cambeak (though the first path on the right, with a white arrow, is a short cut if you prefer). Follow the paths round the headland – where wild goats graze and the views are magnificent – then along the coast back into Crackington Haven.

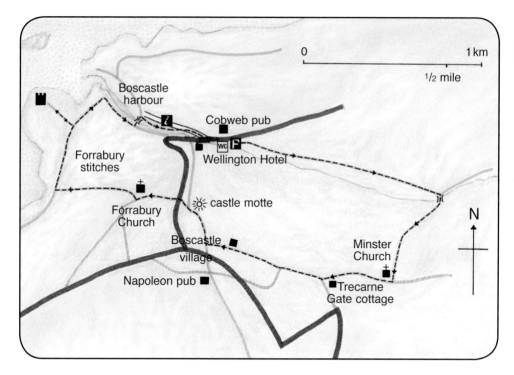

Boscastle
harbour

Cobweb pub

Forrabury
stitches

Wellington Hotel

Forrabury
Church

castle motte

Boscastle
village

Minster
Church

Napoleon pub

Trecarne
Gate cottage

0   1 km

^{1}/$_2$ mile

N

Walk 6   Around Boscastle

Distance: 6 km (nearly 4 miles)   Time: Could be done in 1 ^{1}/$_2$ hours, if you ignored everything of interest on the way! Twice that is more likely. Character: A varied walk with woodland, cliff scenery and one of Cornwall's gems, the village and harbour of Boscastle, now fully recovered from the flood of August 2004. Two steep ascents.

Start from the main car park (SX 100912). Facilities include toilets, several shops, the Cobweb pub, cafés etc. Walk straight across the car park to the slate wall next to the river and turn left to follow a path leading inland up the valley. After 1.3 km turn right across a footbridge (FOOTPATH TO MINSTER CHURCH) and climb the path. Keep right at a fork; the path leads into the churchyard. Minster is the mother church of Boscastle, and it is thought there has been a religious foundation here for 1500 years.

Leave the churchyard by the path uphill, and turn right up the lane. At Trecarne Gate cottage, keep right. After nearly 300 m leave the lane by a stone stile on the right. Go through a field, over a stile and steps, and turn right over another stile. Follow the wire fence on your left and go through a kissing gate on the left. Don't cross the footbridge: continue down the path with the stream on your left.

Gander and Gunnera permitting, cross quietly in front of the house

and walk up the driveway, which leads out onto the main street of the old village, where you turn right. (You may want to make a short diversion for 200 m or so uphill to the second crossroads, above the 'Napoleon', to see some quaint old cottages.)

Descend High Street and, as it veers left, take a path on the right: it soon leads to the Norman motte of Bottreaux Castle, which gave the village its name – not much castle to see, but a lovely outlook.

Continue down the old main street to a fork. Bear left, up to New Road. Turn left and immediately right up FORRABURY HILL. Continue up until, opposite 'Sunny Bank', a short track bears off to the right leading to the simple Norman church of St Symphorian. Notice the old cross outside the churchyard. Go through the churchyard, leaving by the gate at the top left corner; turn left down the track, past the Forrabury stitches – a remarkable survival of medieval strip farming, each strip still individually leased annually.

When you reach the coast path turn right. You will want to visit the white lookout tower, which has rather a good view.

Return to the gateway in the wall which defines the promontory, and turn left. Another time, you might like to try the path which bears off to the right, around the stitches, but this time descend all the way to the harbour. Cross the stream by the Witchcraft Museum and make your way inland to the main road, back to the car park.

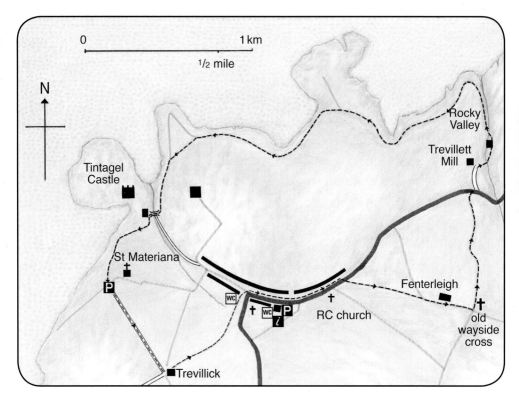

Walk 7 Tintagel and Rocky Valley

Distance: 7.8 km (nearly 5 miles) Time: 2 1/2 hours – but it could be a full day if you visit the castle and church. It can also be combined with walk 8. OS Explorer sheet 111.

Character: One of my favourite walks, avoiding the busiest part of Tintagel village, with superb scenery and generally less crowded than you might expect so close to Tintagel. Very steep climbs.

Start from the Tintagel Visitor Centre (SX 059883) which has explanatory displays; there are public toilets adjoining. From the car park turn right along the main road. Pass the Catholic church and, 40 m beyond Trenale Lane, turn right over a stile (PUBLIC FOOTPATH).

Cross another stile at the end of the hedge on the left of the field. From here the path heads towards a farmhouse called Fenterleigh, three fields away, emerging on a lane – quite a busy one, so take care.

Turn right, up to a crossroads (with an ancient waymark cross) where you turn left (HALGABRON). Continue down this quiet lane, ignoring tempting footpaths, then cross the B3263. The route is signed PUBLIC FOOTPATH TO THE COASTPATH VIA ROCKY VALLEY; pass Trevillett Mill, cross the footbridges and follow the path.

After 200m you will reach the ruins of Trewethet Mill, which contain two maze carvings – possibly Bronze Age but more likely produced in Victorian times by a bored miller – which have become a shrine.

Turn left to cross the stream and follow the path down the far side. Keep left, joining the coast path and climbing steeply.

Follow the coast path west for more than 2 km (very steep in places) till you see Tintagel Haven with the Island and Castle ahead of you. Cross the stream and turn left past the English Heritage shop and exhibition, then immediately bear right up the footpath, COASTPATH – PUBLIC FOOTPATH TREBARWITH STRAND.

Zig-zag up it, turning right at a junction and almost immediately left unless you want to go into the castle – entry fee, but well worth it for the experience – and then keep right and right again.

Climb a stile, then head for Tintagel's isolated Norman church, St Materiana, which repays a proper visit. It contains a Roman milestone.

From the church go through the car park and follow a track parallel to the coast for 550 m till you come to a bungalow at a junction of tracks. Just before the bungalow, turn left over a stone stile along a footpath. Keep to the right of the telephone poles, then diagonally right to another stile, from which a path leads towards the village.

At a path crossing, continue towards the village, cross a wooden bridge then turn left up the road. Just after it bends left, turn right. Emerging on the main street, turn right, back to the Visitor Centre.

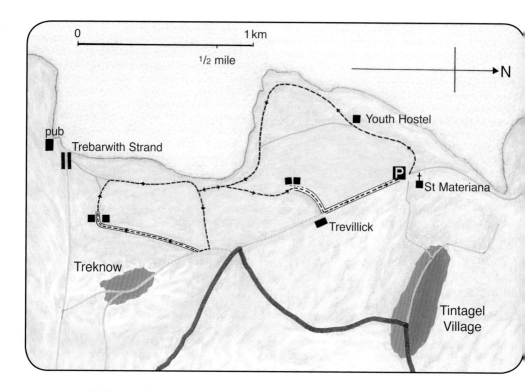

Walk 8   Tintagel and Trebarwith Strand

Distance: 5.2 km (3 1/4 miles)   Time: 1 1/4 hours. It can be combined with walk 7 to make a full day's walk.   OS Explorer sheet 111.
Character: Wonderful cliff scenery, with an inland return. A short and relatively level walk, the easiest in the book.

Park in the cliff car park by St Materiana's church (SX 050884, National Trust, contributions requested). From the church end of the car park, walk along a cart-track (past a bicycle rack) towards the sea. This soon curves left. Stay on the track. At a complex junction of paths, bear right downhill, in the direction of a conical island.

Pass above the Youth Hostel and leave the track by a path to the right, noticing evidence of former slate quarrying, including platforms constructed to hold derricks. Walk round the headland. At a wooden stile and kissing gate turn right and after 50 m cross a stone stile onto Bagalow cliffs.

Before long you will pass the head of a deep gulley, where a wire fence is supported by rectangular slabs of slate. After another 20 m turn left at a stile (notable for a piece of white 'marble' built into it) with a path across a field.

The view over Trebarwith Strand

An abandoned slate quarry on the cliffs just north of Trebarwith Strand, with a grotesque stack of poor quality rock left as a sentinel

Cross this field and the next, then turn right along a lane for 150 m. When the lane bears left, carry straight on along a private road for 600 m. The road or track ends at a group of houses, but a footpath continues downhill towards Trebarwith Strand, a popular cove and beach, with shops, a café, and a pub which has excellent views from its terrace: you may well want to make a diversion at this point!

If not, then at the first junction of paths (unsigned) bear right, then wind uphill to a T-junction of paths. Turn right, and follow the coast path for 650 m past some extraordinary pillars of rock: the slate here was presumably of inferior quality and so rejected.

When you arrive back at the stile with the white 'marble', continue for just 20 m. Where the coast path turns left along the cliff edge, keep straight on (TREVILLICK) beside the wall. Cross two fields, then follow a track straight ahead past the white houses.

At Trevillick crossroads, turn left (TO THE COASTPATH) along a minor road which leads back to the church and your car.

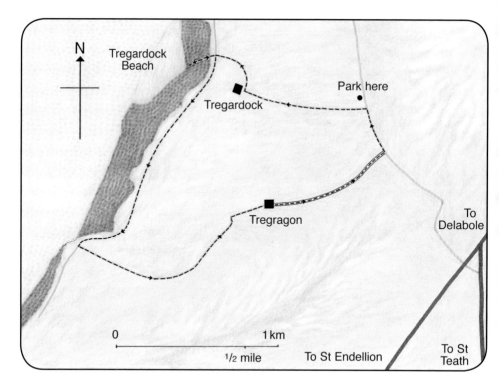

Walk 9   Tregardock Beach

Distance: 6.3 km (4 miles)   Time: 2 hours   OS Explorer sheet 111
Character: Superb cliffs (care needed with children and dogs),
a wonderful expanse of beach (at low tide) and a pleasant inland
return. Several steep ascents and descents.

Parking: one mile south from Delabole, turn right to TRELIGGA. After
1 km, just beyond the left turn to Tregardock, there is parking for 4
cars (SX 053838).

For this walk, there is no point in parking down the lane to Tregardock, which becomes very congested in summer with people going to
the beach. You will not shorten the walk that way.

Walk down the lane. Just before the farm entrance, turn right
through a gate, TO THE COASTPATH. After 200 m bear left at a path
junction. Before long a gate leads you onto Tregardock Cliffs (National
Trust).

When you reach a crossroads of paths, carry straight on to Tregardock Beach, which even at high tide is well worth a visit for its scenic
qualities. At low tide there is plenty of room for everyone: the long
walk back to the car tends to deter families with young children.

Return uphill to the 'crossroads' and turn right along the coastpath until you come to a little footbridge. Ignore the stile on your left (unless you need a short cut) and begin a major descent. At the bottom, before the stream, turn left across a stile, heading up a wild and deserted valley. *

After two gates, a better defined path leads steadily uphill: it's quite a long drag! At the top turn left over a stile and immediately right over another one.

Head for the farm. Cross a stile, then walk between the farm buildings; follow a concrete drive gently uphill till you reach a tarmac lane. Turn left, and in 300 m you will reach your car.

---

* You could now choose to extend your walk south along the coastpath for as long as you like, returning later to this point. To help you decide: from here back to your car is 2.5 km (1½ miles), including a longish ascent, taking perhaps 45 minutes.

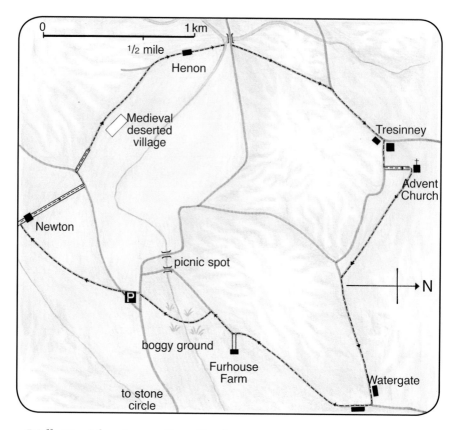

Walk 10   Advent, near Camelford

Distance: 8.2km (5 miles) Time: 2¹/₂ hours OS Explorer sheet 109
Character: Moorland edge, where farming is a tough business.
Includes a deserted medieval village, and an unspoiled old church.
No significant hills, but innumerable stiles and some uneven walking.
The paths may be overgrown with nettles, so don't go bare-legged.

Start at Harpur's Downs. To get there from Camelford, take the lane
from Tregoodwell (at the north end of the town) towards Roughtor,
and turn right at a crossroads, signed ADVENT CHURCH.

At two junctions keep left then follow a narrow lane till you cross
a stream – a picnic spot. At a T-junction turn left. After 300m, there
is a triangle of grass at a road junction. Park here (SX 115798). When
you've done the walk, don't miss the stone circle at SX 126800; drive
towards, then past, the Stannon china clay works; the circle lies on the
right just beyond where the tarmac gives out.

Start the walk by following a path south-west, away from the china
clay pits, towards a stile in a wall with a yellow arrow on it. (After very

22

wet weather, you may want to stick to the lane. See map.) Cross 5 stiles, then pass through a wood and emerge via a stile onto an old track. Turn right up it, past a farm (Newton) and on up to a lane.

Turn left, and after 80 m, when the lane bends, take the track straight on (PUBLIC FOOTPATH) through a gate and through a yard, then up a holloway (a medieval track) which leads to and through the deserted village of Carwether. At the top of the slope its ruins are clearly visible as humps and bumps to the right of the track. The village has gone but its right-of-way remains! Notice where it broadens at the village centre.

Follow the holloway down, keeping to the left when it gets over-grown, and through a wooden gate. At a barn, keep right and pass through Henon to cross a stream by a clapper bridge. Cross the lane and take the PUBLIC FOOTPATH opposite, through a gate. Keep the hedge to your right across two fields, then straight across the third, which brings you to a lane: turn right up the lane to the hamlet of Tresinney. At the road junction turn right and after 100 m turn left, signed ADVENT CHURCH. Turn right into the churchyard.

Leave the churchyard by a stile at the far (east) end – continue straight across the field, don't turn right. Follow waymarked stiles over 5 fields. Leave by a stile (not the gate) and turn left along the lane.

After 1 km at a junction turn right, then after 1.2 km (200 m beyond the entrance to Furhouse Farm) turn left across a stile (PUBLIC FOOTPATH). Head through the glade (the ruins of a settlement) and descend the slope, keeping close to the hedge on your left. Cross a boggy area by stepping stones then follow the waymarked path, which will bring you to your car.

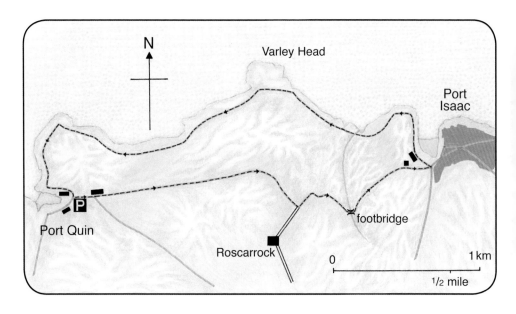

Walk 11 Port Quin to Port Isaac

Distance: 8km (5 miles)   Time: 2¹/₂ hours plus time at Port Isaac
OS Explorer 106

Character: Initially quiet rural, then a delightful view of Port Isaac,
then a magnificent coastal section. Very steep ascents and descents,
many steps. A demanding walk.

Park in the National Trust car park at Port Quin (donations requested
– and well deserved for the work they do along this coast) at SS 972805.

Leave the car park by the vehicle entrance, turn right and walk up
the lane for 150 m. Bear left across the front of the cottages (PUBLIC
FOOTPATH PORT ISAAC 2). From a stile, this is an easily followed path
then track through a landscape of broad rolling fields.

Pass through 3 gateways (with stiles, but the gates are often open).
At the fourth gateway, some 200 m before you reach Roscarrock farm,
the track turns right, but you instead go through the gateway and turn
left towards the sea, alongside the hedge and round the field border
to a stile.

Descend into the valley bottom to a footbridge. Take the path uphill
on the far side. Emerging from the bushes, head straight up to and
past an old lookout post: there's a stile one third of the way up the
far hedge. From the next field there are wonderful views of Port Isaac
– but don't go too far! Your path lies just beside the left hedge, and
becomes a holloway – an old track worn down by centuries of horses

so that it turns into a watercourse in winter, and is muddy even in summer. It brings you to the edge of Port Isaac.

You need to turn left onto the coastal path – but it would be surprising if you didn't want to explore Port Isaac first.

The return along the coast path requires no directions: just proceed for 5 km. It is quite tough going but the scenery will sustain you.

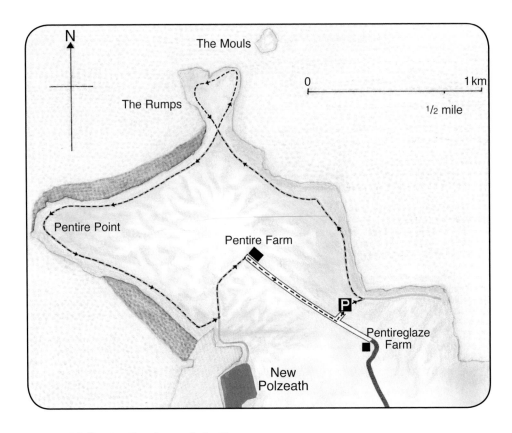

Walk 12   Pentire and the Rumps

Distance: 6.5 km (4 miles)   Time: 2 hours   OS Explorer Sheet 106
Character: Superb cliff scenery, and only a short inland stretch.

Park at the National Trust car park just beyond Pentireglaze (SW 941800). To get there, take the POLZEATH/PORT QUIN turning off the B 3314, pass the Bee Centre and keep right. At the next junction fork right, NEW POLZEATH.

Then take the second turning on the right (at a crossroads), drive through Pentireglaze farm, and take the first car park offered on the right. This is in fact on the site of a former lead mine.

Leave by the path past the contributions box up over some spoil heaps and across a small field. Go through the gate and turn left along the coast path. On a clear day you can see as far as Hartland Point, over 50 km (30 miles) away. After 500 m you will see ahead of you 'the Rumps': the name derives from the Anglo-Saxon and is not Cornish! It is a distinctive double headland which was fortified in the Iron Age. Cross the outer ditch and rampart at a gateway.

Explore the area whichever way you like, but a walk around the right buttock gives perhaps the most interesting views, of rock formations and an island called The Mouls. However, the view from the top of the left buttock is more extensive. Return to the gateway and turn right, which will lead you to Pentire Point and on to Pentire Haven, where the path skirts a deep sandy inlet.

From the head of the cove a path leads inland up the valley. On reaching slate-hung Pentire Farm, turn right up the track which will lead you back to your car.

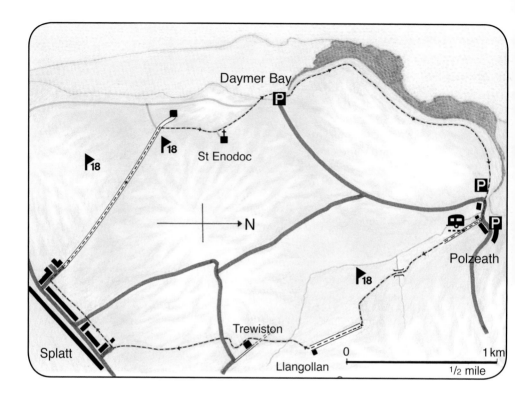

Walk 13   Polzeath and Daymer Bay

Distance: 8.7 km (5¹/₂ miles)   Time: 2¹/₄ hours.   OS Explorer sheet 106 Character: A pleasant easy walk if you're staying in Polzeath or Rock, consisting of farmland, golf courses, estuary and seashore. Beaches and rockpools for the young at heart. Take care within the golf courses.

From the beach at Polzeath (SW 937789) take the private road inland to the left of the stream, signed to a caravan park. Pass between the caravan park and a row of elevated bungalows, and up a track. Cross a stream, then after 30 m go forward at a path crossing to enter a golf course, climbing and keeping an old hedgebank on your right.

Continue in the same direction across the fairways; when you reach the hedge keep left along it for 130 m, then turn right up a waymarked path, to the centre of this golf course complex, once Llangollan farm. When you come to a wall, turn left and immediately right at a 'cross-roads', taking the footpath ahead, signed PUBLIC FOOTPATH, bearing slightly right, to find a stile in a tall hedge.

Leaving the golf course the path cuts diagonally across the corner of a field to a stile, then across the next field in the same direction.

28

Cross the farm yard, following the FOOTPATH sign. Once into a field, turn left and follow the field edge to a stone stile. Cross a narrow field in the same direction, turn right at the hedge and in 30 m turn left. Cross to the far right corner of the camping field, where a stile leads into a lane. Cross the lane.

The footpath continues across four more fields (the exit from the second is at 'one o'clock' but if the path has not been re-established you may need to go along two sides of the field, keeping the hedge on your left) and out onto a track between houses in the village of Splatt.

After 50 m of the track, turn right where there is a black metal bollard with dog-fouling notices on it, past Manor Cottage along a back alley and then over a stone stile into a field. Cross a road – Trewint Lane – and continue up the lane opposite, which soon becomes a track. At a crossroads, turn right past a few bungalows and out along a tarmac track which leads to and through a picturesque golf links.

Some 150 m short of a glade of trees, bear right off the track (way-marked) across a stone bridge. Turn left and follow the white stones. Cross the fairway and walk to its left. Circle around the green to visit St Enodoc's church. From here the path becomes a track. When it forks, bear left and follow the white stone markers till you reach the beach: turn right along it.

Go up the steps and turn left across the front of the Daymer Bay car park, where the facilities include a shop and toilets, and follow the coast path for 1.6km back to Polzeath.

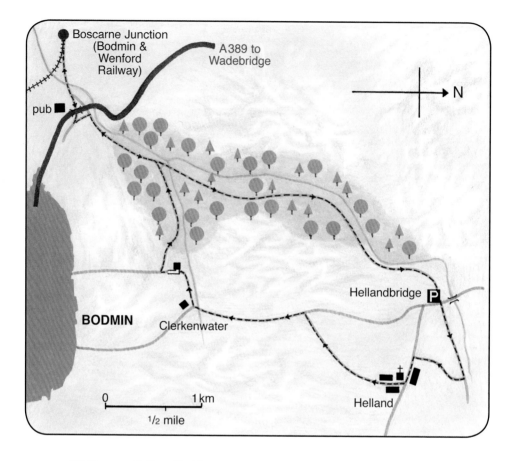

Walk 14   Hellandbridge to Dunmere

Distance: 10.5 km (6½ miles) Time: 2½ hours OS Explorer sheet 109
The extension to Boscarne Junction and back adds 4 km (2½ miles)
and takes an extra hour. This walk can alternatively be done from
Boscarne Junction, reached by preserved steam railway from Bodmin.

Character: Different from the other walks in this book: a little longer –
much longer if you include Boscarne – but very easy walking, relatively
flat, almost entirely on hard surfaces (tracks and some very quiet lanes)
with few stiles. An attractive inland walk through pleasant
farming country, then wonderful mixed woodland.

Park at Hellandbridge (SX065714). From the car park, which was a
wharf on the old railway line, cross the lane and proceed east along
the Camel Trail for 1 km. At some farm buildings, turn right up a
lane passing through the hamlet of Bodwen. At a T-junction turn left.
After 300 m turn right at the war memorial, go through the attractive

hamlet of Helland, and continue for 1.2 km until you reach a T-junction, where you turn left. After 1 km, at the bottom of a hill and just before a roadside cottage ('Old Laundry') turn right along an unsigned track.

Keep left at a fork after 400 m. Climb to and past Copshorn farm: the track becomes tarmac. Nearing the top of the slope turn right through a gate along a track, passing a solar farm, which leads into woodland, through another gate.

Immediately turn left down a lesser used path. At the next junction (a broad glade) continue downhill. You will soon reach a cross-track which runs parallel to the Camel Trail. At this point you can turn right and join

the Trail in 100 m or so, and it will take you back to Hellandbridge.

However, you can make an interesting extension by keeping left, and joining the Trail after a further 500 m. At a sign CAMEL TRAIL BODMIN & WADEBRIDGE, turn left. (To go straight on here is possible, and saves perhaps 300 m, but it brings you to a seriously dangerous road crossing.) Follow the track left for 350 m, then double back right (PADSTOW WADEBRIDGE) along the disused railway line.

This was the Bodmin & Wadebridge, one of the earliest steam railways in the world, opened in 1834. If you proceed past the defunct platform of Dunmere Junction (with access to the Borough Arms pub) for another 600 m you will reach Boscarne Junction. It is served by the steam trains of the Bodmin & Wenford Railway.

The return to Hellandbridge is simplicity itself: just follow the Camel Trail for 6 km through some lovely woodland.

Some other Bossiney titles

King Arthur – man or myth?
King Arthur's footsteps
Discover north Cornwall
About Tintagel

Really short walks – north Cornwall (3-5km)
Shortish walks: Bodmin Moor (6-8km)
Shortish walks: Lower Tamar Valley (5-9km)
Really short walks – St Ives to Padstow (3-6km)

Discover Dartmoor
Really short walks to explore Dartmoor (2-6km)
Shortish walks on Dartmoor (6-8km)
Fairly easy walks on Dartmoor (3-9km)
Shortish walks in north Devon (5-9km)
Fairly easy walks in north Devon (3-8km)

We have a comprehensive selection of walks books
covering Cornwall, Devon and Exmoor – please see our website
www.bossineybooks.com